Contents

Fiction
Red Zone
page 2

Non-fiction
Simulation
page 18

Written by
David Clayton
Illustrated by
Peter Richardson

Series editor **Dee Reid**

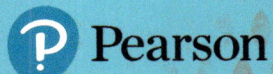

Before reading Red Zone

Characters

Joe

Man in a silver suit

Lady in a dark suit

Tricky words

- building
- decided
- through
- corridor
- disappeared
- swipe
- autopilot
- simulator

Read these words to the student. Help them with these words when they appear in the text.

Introduction

Joe knew there was something strange going on in Moon City but he didn't know what. He saw a bus stop next to a tall building and people in silver suits got off the bus and went in the building. Joe decided to follow them. He found himself in a long empty corridor. Then he saw a swipe card on the floor. Was this his chance to find out what's going on in Moon City?

Red Zone

Joe was thinking hard. He was trying to work things out. Something strange was going on in Moon City but he didn't know what.
A bus stopped next to a tall building.
Joe saw people in silver suits get off the bus and go into the building. He decided to follow them. He slipped through the door just as it closed.

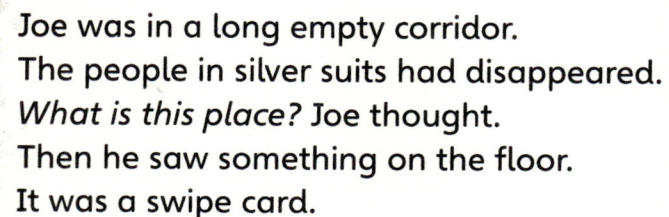

Joe was in a long empty corridor.
The people in silver suits had disappeared.
What is this place? Joe thought.
Then he saw something on the floor.
It was a swipe card.

Just then, Joe heard someone coming.
He had to hide!
He saw a swipe card slot in the wall by a door. He swiped the card in the slot and the door opened. Joe stepped inside.
He looked through a crack in the door.
A lady in a silver suit was walking past.
Joe closed the door.
That was close, he thought.

Joe turned around. "Wow!" he gasped. He was looking at a huge rocket. *I'm going to look inside it*, he thought. *This might be my chance to find out what is going on in Moon City.*

Joe climbed into the pilot's seat. All around him were dials and switches.

He pulled on the pilot's headset, but as he did this, he knocked one of the switches.

Joe felt the rocket move. He was tipped back and he could see the roof above him opening.

"30 seconds to take off…" said a voice in the headset. "20…15…10…"
"Hang on!" shouted Joe. "I can't fly this thing! Help!"
But the voice went on, "…6…5…4…3…2…1!"
BOOM!
The kick of the engine pinned Joe to his seat. The rocket zoomed into space at amazing speed, leaving Moon City far behind.

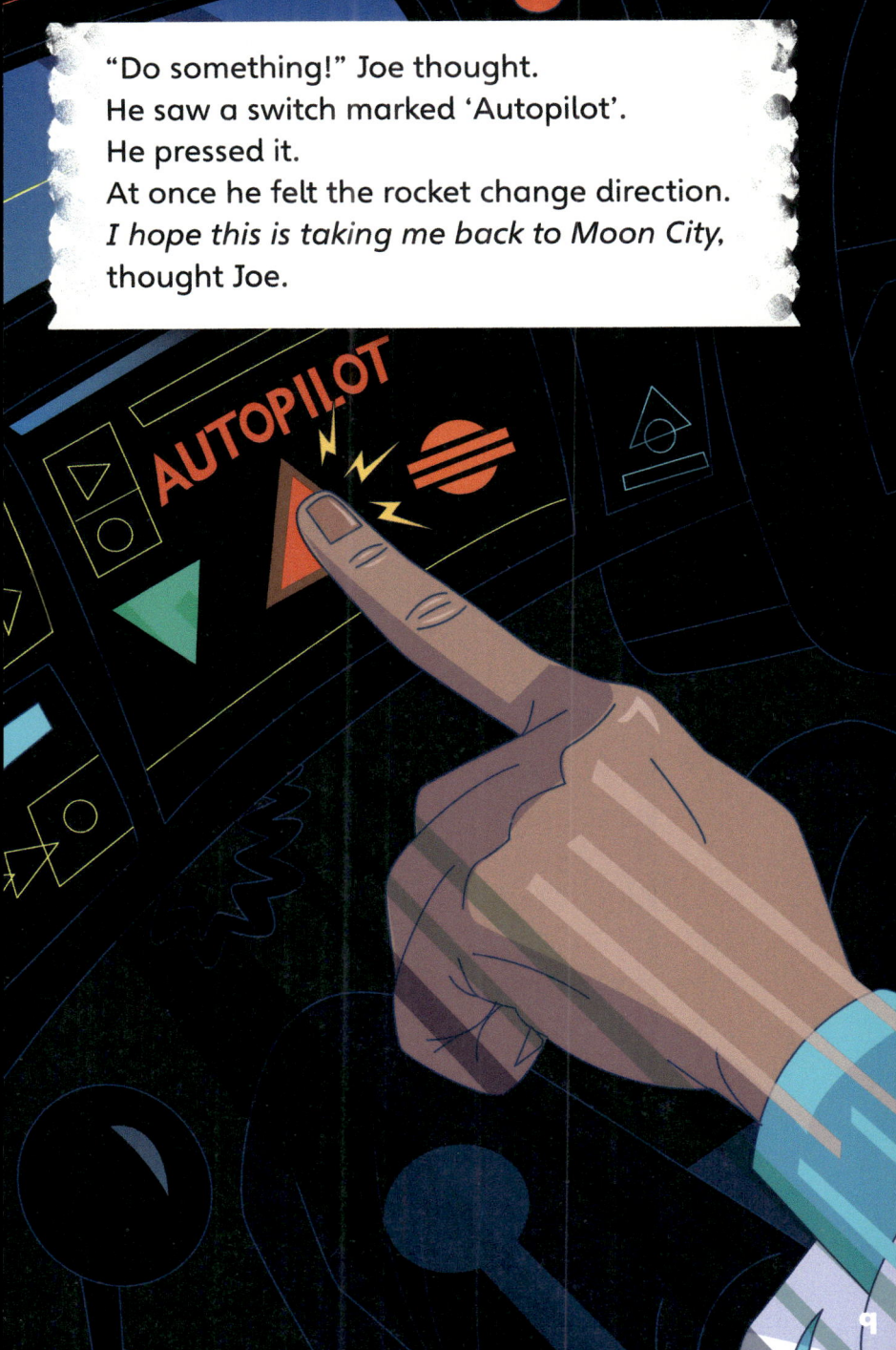

"Do something!" Joe thought.
He saw a switch marked 'Autopilot'.
He pressed it.
At once he felt the rocket change direction.
I hope this is taking me back to Moon City, thought Joe.

But then he saw a huge planet in front of him. He knew what it was. It was Earth.
The rocket was flying straight towards Earth!
At that moment, Joe heard the voice in his headset say, "Rocket on target. Impact on New York in 30 seconds! 20…15…"
They were going to crash!
Joe looked around him. He had to do something quickly or he was going to destroy New York. He pulled back hard on a control stick next to him but nothing happened. He was still speeding towards the Earth.

Joe's heart was thumping.
Here it comes! he thought.
He closed his eyes and covered his head with his hands.

Then Joe saw a man in a silver suit standing over him.
"What are you doing in there?" shouted the man. "This is a Red Zone Restricted Area. What did you see?"
The man's angry face was getting redder and redder but all Joe could think was, *I'm alive!*

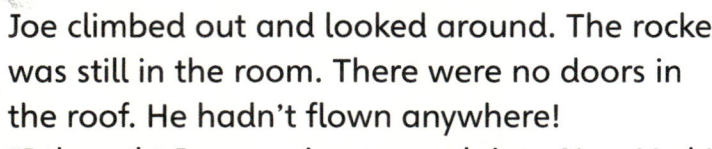

Joe climbed out and looked around. The rocket was still in the room. There were no doors in the roof. He hadn't flown anywhere!

"I thought I was going to crash into New York!" said Joe.

"It's just a simulator," shouted the man. "But you shouldn't be in here anyway. How did you get in?"

Joe showed him the swipe card. "It was on the floor," he said.

The man grabbed the card. His red face suddenly went pale. The swipe card was his. "Get out of here," he shouted. "But if you tell anyone about what you have seen, you will wish you **had** died in a rocket crash."

Then the man grabbed Joe and shoved him outside.

Just as Joe was getting to his feet, a lady in a dark suit came up to him.
"Keep away from here, it's dangerous," she hissed.
"What do you mean?" said Joe, but the lady had walked off.

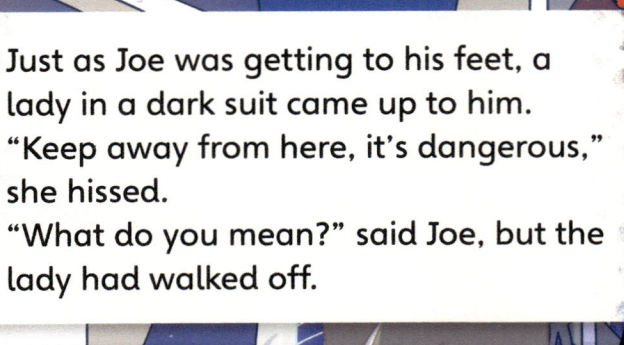

Joe's head was buzzing. *What was all that about and why was a simulator programmed to destroy New York?* There were strange things going on in Moon City…

Quiz

Text comprehension

Literal comprehension
p5 How did Joe get into the rocket room?
p14 Had Joe really been about to crash into New York?

Inferential comprehension
p10 Why did nothing happen when Joe pulled on the control stick?
p11 What did Joe think was going to happen when he thinks *Here it comes!*?
p15 Why did the man go pale when he realised it was his swipe card?

Personal response
- Would you have dared get into the pilot's seat?
- Who do you think the lady in the dark suit is?

Word knowledge

p3 Find a word that means 'weird'.
p10 Why is there an exclamation mark after 'Earth' on the third line?
p15 Find two verbs which show that the man was angry.

Spelling challenge

Read these words:

suddenly   through   nothing

Now try to spell them!

Ha! Ha! Ha!

What is an astronaut's favourite part of a computer?

The Space bar!

Before reading *Simulation*

Find out about

- how computers can be used to imitate things that happen in real life.

Tricky words

- simulation
- imitate
- using
- parachute
- operate
- virtual
- patients
- character

Read these words to the student. Help them with these words when they appear in the text.

Introduction

Simulation is when we use computers to imitate things that happen in real life. We can use a simulator to do things that are dangerous or difficult for us to do in real life. Simulation can be used to try parachute jumping or driving a Formula One racing car.

Simulation

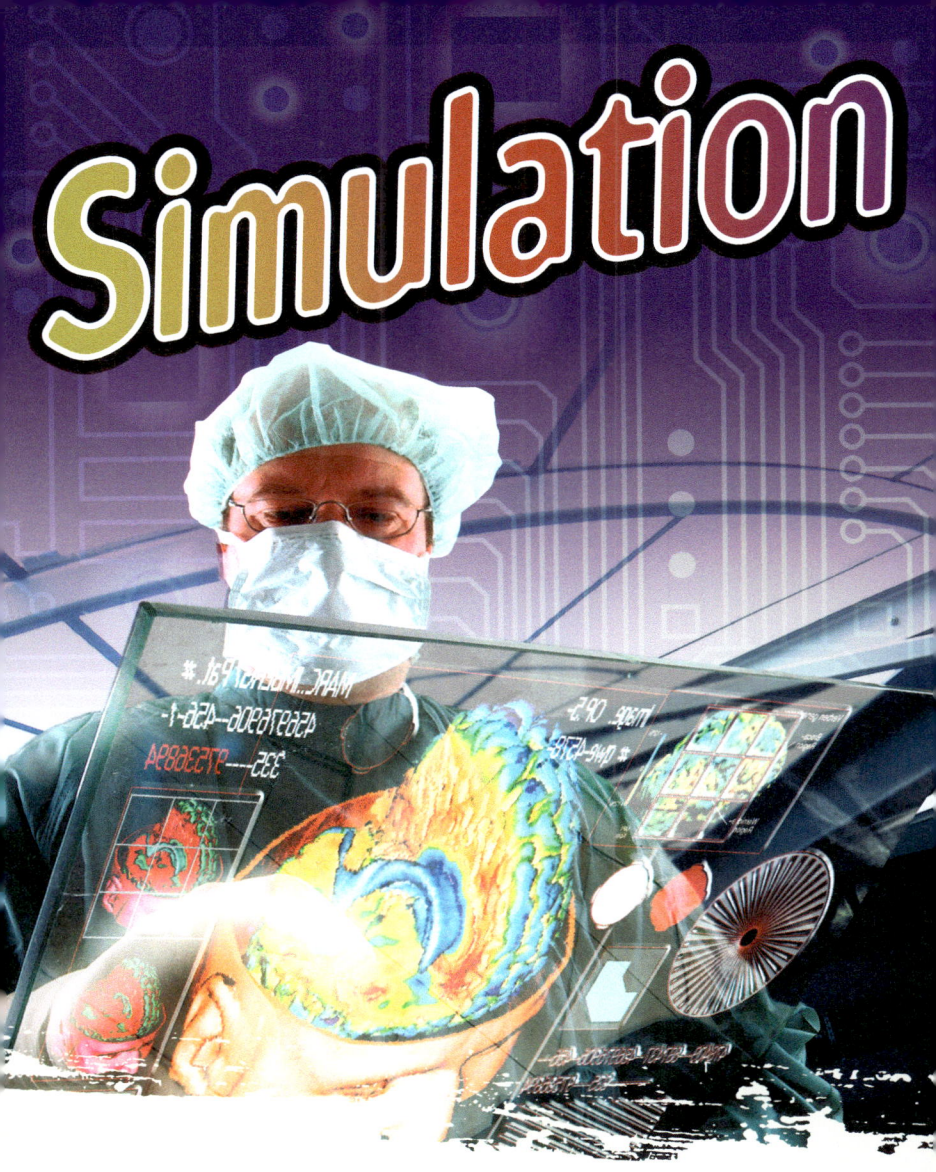

Simulation is when we use computers to imitate things that happen in real life.
Why do we need simulation?
Why don't we just do things in real life?

There are some things that are too dangerous or difficult for us to do in real life unless we are experts.
Using simulation, we can learn how to do dangerous things in a safe way.
Simulation can be used to learn a skill or it can be used for fun.
Most of us can't do free-fall parachute jumping.
Most of us can't drive a Formula One racing car.
But we **can** do these things in a simulator.

When people are training to be doctors they sometimes use simulators to learn how to help patients. Everything they see and touch feels real, but really it is just on the computer! Doctors can even operate on virtual patients. They can find out what it is like to cut someone open and operate on them before they start to cut up a real person! Using simulation helps them to avoid making mistakes with real patients.

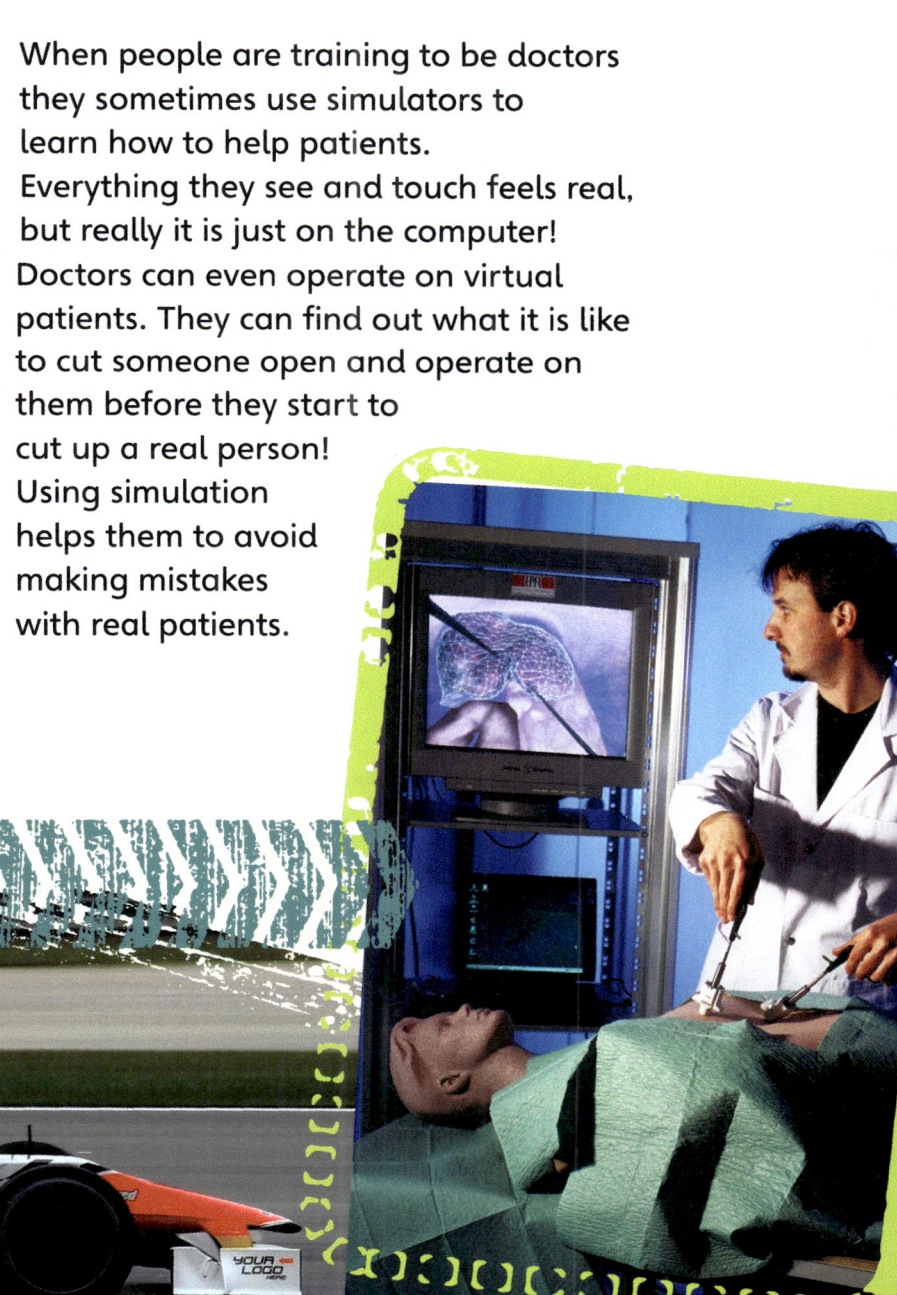

When people are training to be pilots they use simulators to learn how to fly planes. The simulator makes the person feel as if they are in a cockpit and flying a real plane.

Airlines also use simulators to check that pilots are doing their jobs properly. The simulator can test that they know what to do if they have a problem. They show the pilot a problem and the pilot can practise what he would do to stop the plane from crashing. It is a good way to make air travel as safe as possible.

Drivers use simulators to practise driving Formula One cars.
The controls are the same as in a real car.
The track on the screen is the same as the real track they will be racing on.
The track can be made slippery. This allows them to learn how to control a car on a wet track.

Driving simulators can also be used for fun.
You can find out what it is like to drive a
racing car when you play a driving computer game.
You can feel what it is like to travel at 100 miles
an hour and race against other cars.
And, of course, if you crash, you don't get hurt.

In Nintendo Wii games you use a steering wheel to make it feel like you are really driving the car. When you turn the wheel, the car turns. If you turn too sharply the car will spin out of control.

You can also use the Wii to simulate sports such as bowling, golf and tennis. You hold the remote and swing your arm as if you were really playing that sport and your character on the screen copies your movements.

Watch out though – if you are not careful you can cause 'wiinjuries' if you let go and your remote hits someone! Ouch!

The Xbox Kinect simulates things without a remote.
You play these games just by moving your body.
You do not even need a steering wheel for driving games.

As well as simulation games, you can use computers to simulate another life...

On the website Second Life, you can create an avatar for yourself and live a second life on the internet. You can make a life for yourself that might seem better than your real life. You might have more money or more friends. You can make friends with other avatars and do anything you can do in real life.

When you create your avatar you can choose what you want to look like. For example, if you have long brown hair in real life, you can make your avatar have short blonde hair. Some people find they like their avatar's life even more than they like their real life! This could be a problem because although things look very real on the website, they are not real.

But sometimes what has happened in simulations can happen in real life. There are some people whose avatars have met on Second Life and then they have got married in real life!

Quiz

Text comprehension

Literal comprehension
p20 How can simulation be useful?
p28 What's special about the Xbox Kinect?

Inferential comprehension
p22 How do simulators help air safety?
p24 Which is more important – simulation for skills or for fun?
p30 Why might spending a lot of time on Second Life not be a good idea?

Personal response
- Have you ever played a simulation game?
- Would you be interested in the Second Life website?

Word knowledge

p20 Why is the word 'can' in bold?
p25 Find two adverbs on this page.
p30 Find a word that means 'life-like'.

Spelling challenge

Read these words:

yourself   impossible   although

Now try to spell them!

Ha! Ha! Ha!

How do astronauts keep in touch?

Through Spacebook!